ODELL BECKHAM JR.

PRO BOWL WIDE RECEIVER

RYAN NAGELHOUT

Britannica
Educational Publishing

IN ASSOCIATION WITH

ROSEN
EDUCATIONAL SERVICES

Published in 2019 by Britannica Educational Publishing (a trademark of Encyclopædia Britannica, Inc.) in association with The Rosen Publishing Group, Inc.
29 East 21st Street, New York, NY 10010

Distributed exclusively by Rosen Publishing.
To see additional Britannica Educational Publishing titles, go to rosenpublishing.com.

First Edition

Britannica Educational Publishing
J.E. Luebering: Executive Director, Core Editorial
Andrea R. Field: Managing Editor, Compton's by Britannica

Rosen Publishing
Kathy Kuhtz Campbell: Senior Editor
Nelson Sá: Art Director
Nicole Russo-Duca: Series Designer and Book Layout
Cindy Reiman: Photography Manager
Sherri Jackson: Photo Researcher

Library of Congress Cataloging-in-Publication Data

Names: Nagelhout, Ryan, author.
Title: Odell Beckham Jr.: Pro Bowl wide receiver / Ryan Nagelhout.
Description: New York: Britannica Educational Publishing, in Association with Rosen Educational Services, 2019. | Series: Living legends of sports | Includes bibliographical references and index. | Audience: Grades 5–8.
Identifiers: LCCN 2017049257| ISBN 9781680488715 (library bound) | ISBN 9781538302095 (pbk.)
Subjects: LCSH: Beckham, Odell, Jr., 1992– —Juvenile literature. | Football
Players—United States—Biography—Juvenile literature. | New York Giants
(Football team)—History—Juvenile literature.
Classification: LCC GV939.B424 N34 2019 | DDC 796.332092 [B]—dc23
LC record available at https://lccn.loc.gov/2017049257

Manufactured in the United States of America

Photo credits: Cover, p. 1 Justin K. Aller/Getty Images; cover and interior pages background © iStockphoto.com/Traffic Analyzer; pp. 4-5, 25, 37 Al Bello/Getty Images; p. 7 Roberto Michel/Shutterstock.com; p. 8 Rommel Demano/Getty Images; p. 10 Collegiate Images/Getty Images; pp. 12-13 John Biever/Sports Illustrated/Getty Images; p. 14bSean Gardner/Getty Images; pp. 17, 18 Icon Sports Wire/Getty Images; p. 20 New York Daily News/Getty Images; p. 21 Elsa/Getty Images; p. 22 Photo by Frank Micelotta /Invision for NFL/AP Images; pp. 26-27 Tim Clayton/Corbis Sport/Getty Images; pp. 28-29 Brad Barket/Getty Images; p. 30 Michael Reaves/Getty Images; p. 31 Stacy Revere/Getty Images; p. 33 Angel Martinez/Real Madrid/Getty Images; p. 35 Joe Scarnici /WireImage/Getty Images; p. 36 Rich Schultz/Getty Images; p. 38 Steven Ryan/Getty Images.

CONTENTS

INTRO-DUCTION

O dell Beckham Jr. is known for many things in his brief but illustrious career in the National Football League (NFL). After a brilliant career at Louisiana State University (LSU) he burst onto the NFL scene as a rookie for the New York Giants. His colossal individual performances as a receiver soon made him a national sensation.

Among the highlights of Beckham's pro career was a spectacular one-handed catch that he made on TV's *Sunday Night Football* during his rookie season in 2014. People marveled at his ability on the field. But he also began to get scrutiny for actions other than his impressive playmaking.

In 2016, Beckham was named by the *Sporting News* as one of the "most hated" players in the NFL. In just four seasons, his career has been filled with drama and excellence. But why? The perception of Beckham, as brilliant as he has been on the field, is that he also is a troublemaker. Many fans think he complains. He has started fights with other players, shown his frustration and anger on the field, and caused headaches for his coaches and team with his touchdown celebrations.

Beckham's catch on *Sunday Night Football* against the Dallas Cowboys in 2014 has gone down as one of the best catches in NFL history.

On the field, when the ball is snapped, there are few receivers better than Beckham. Here is how Seattle Seahawks cornerback Richard Sherman described Beckham during his rookie year in 2014. One of the best defenders of the last decade, Sherman has seen his fair share of talented wideouts (as wide receivers are also known) and broke them down in a piece for the *Players' Tribune* in 2016. He started his analysis by talking about Beckham in a game they played two weeks before his famous catch against the Cowboys on November 23, 2014.

In that Week 10 game against the Giants, I had been out on the field for a few plays when Odell came in fresh off the bench. He ran a stop-and-go, and I had it covered pretty well. When he made his first cut, I was right in his pocket.

Then he came out of the second part of his break, and he just exploded—like he had been shot out of a cannon—and he caught the ball for a big gain.

I was like, O.K. Now I know.

No one can deny Odell Beckham Jr.'s ability on the field. But there is much more to Beckham than one extraordinary catch against the Dallas Cowboys or a touchdown celebration that upsets fans. The son of athletes grew up to be an athlete himself, and a remarkable one. But his growth as a player—and a person—is what makes his young career so interesting.

Growing Up a Tiger

Odell Beckham Jr. was born in Baton Rouge, Louisiana, on November 5, 1992. Sports were a constant in his family. His father, Odell Beckham Sr., was a star running back in high school. His mother, Heather Van Norman, was a track standout. Both athletes attended LSU, where they first met.

Tiger Stadium at Louisiana State University (LSU) in Baton Rouge is home to Tiger football. Odell Beckham Sr. was a running back for the Tigers.

Odell Beckham Jr. (*right*) poses with his mother, Heather Van Norman, at a charity event. Heather was a track star when she was a student at LSU.

Odell Sr. played running back for the LSU football team for three seasons, from 1989 to 1992. Heather was a track star there as well. Later in life, Beckham's mother went on to coach track in college. He said his mother would often send him tips about his running, even when he was in college himself.

"She's been a track coach for a while. I remember her texting me after games. I had decent games, and she's texting me—'Oh, your form looks great,'" Beckham said to reporters in 2014. "It's funny to hear coming from her. She's a track coach. It's not like, 'That's a nice catch.' She's talking about running form."

> ## QUICK FACT
>
> Odell Beckham Sr. was so good in high school he was mentioned in a famous football book. He attended Marshall High School in Texas and played against the Permian Panthers team featured in Buzz Bissinger's 1990 book *Friday Night Lights.*

Odell Jr. is the oldest of three children. He has a younger brother, Kordell, and a younger sister named Jasmine. Sports and athletes were a huge influence on Odell's life growing up. Another LSU sports star, basketball player Shaquille O'Neal, acted like an uncle to him while he was growing up.

Following Footsteps

Odell went to high school in New Orleans, and he excelled as an athlete at a young age. He played football and basketball and ran track at Isidore Newman High School. Odell was one of the most talented players on his football team, so he played many different positions— wide receiver, quarterback, running back, and cornerback.

He had some very impressive statistics in high school. During his senior year, he caught 50 passes for 1,010 yards and 19 touchdowns; he also ran for 331 yards and six touchdowns, passed for an additional touchdown, and scored on two punt returns. In 2011, Odell was selected to play in the US Army All-American Bowl, a showcase for some of the

Beckham played for the LSU Tigers as a freshman and was productive as a wide receiver. His best performances came as a junior.

best high school football players in the nation. He won first team honors for Louisiana's 2A All-Star team as a wideout.

This honor got him a lot of attention from college coaches who wanted him to play for their team. According to Rivals.com, Odell was the sixth-best high-school receiver in the country when he accepted a scholarship offer to play at LSU. Odell was recruited by many other schools. But Beckham wanted to play for his parents' school, and the LSU Tigers were eager to have him join the team.

Tigers Pride

Unlike many college football players, Beckham made an immediate impact on the field. He played as a true freshman in his first season with the team, starting his first game against the Oregon Ducks on September 3, 2011. Three weeks later, Beckham scored his first collegiate touchdown in a game against West Virginia. He started in nine of 14 games his freshman year, and LSU had a very good season. They made the Bowl Championship Series (BCS) National Championship Game, but the Tigers lost to the Alabama Crimson Tide, 21–0. Beckham did have five catches for 38 yards in the loss. Overall, his freshman year was a success. He had 41 catches for 475 yards and two touchdowns and was named to the All-Southeastern Conference (SEC) team.

The 2012 season saw a much bigger role for Beckham on the Tigers, as he shone both as a punt returner and as a wideout. He returned his first career collegiate punt for a touchdown against North Texas to open the season and built on that to get his first ever 100-yard game against Towson on September 29. His 128 yards came on five catches, and he had two touchdowns on that day (LSU won 38–22). LSU's offense was powered by Beckham and future NFL standout Jarvis Landry, who led the team in receiving in 2012. Beckham finished behind Landry with 713 receiving yards on 43 catches, but the two were primed to have a significant junior season together.

Beckham reached the BCS National Championship Game with LSU in 2012, though the Tigers lost to Alabama in the title game.

"Don't Blink"

Beckham had his best season as a junior (2013–14) at LSU. The 5-feet-11-inch wideout excelled while playing with Landry, creating one of the most dominant wideout combinations in SEC history. LSU quarterback Zach Mettenberger raved about having two big targets to throw to in Beckham's junior season.

"The great thing for a quarterback is that one of them always seems to be open," Mettenberger said to Chris Low of ESPN in 2013. "If you try to take one of them away, the other one's going to get you."

Landry said being able to work closely with Beckham over their time at LSU made them both better.

"Because we're so close, we have the ability to critique each other and push each other, whether it be in practice or wherever," Landry told Low. "Odell's got great speed, vision with the ball and the yards after the catch, and my strength is catching the ball and being physical. I'm always taking something out of his book or

QUICK FACT

Jarvis Landry had slightly more receiving yards than Beckham during his junior season: 1,193 compared to Beckham's 1,152. He also had more touchdowns: 10 compared to Beckham's eight.

helping him with something I do well to complement his game."

Mettenberger, Beckham, Landry, and running back Jeremy Hill combined to form one of the best offenses in LSU history. The Tigers were the first SEC team to have a 3,000-yard passer, a 1,000-yard rusher, and two 1,000-yard receivers play in the same season.

Beckham raved about Landry as well and said the duo made them must-see TV when LSU played in a big game.

"We told each other that our motto this year was going to be, 'Don't blink,'" Beckham told Low. "That's because if you're at home watching on TV and step away for a second, you might miss an exciting play."

One of the most exciting plays that season was a 109-yard return for a touchdown when the University of Alabama Birmingham (UAB) missed a long field goal. Beckham caught the missed field goal nine yards deep in the end zone and raced down the field to score the touchdown.

His speed as a kick returner made Beckham a big target in the NFL Draft.

Moving On

In his junior season, Beckham led the SEC in all-purpose yards and was second in the nation, with an average of 178.1 yards per game. He finished with 1,152 receiving yards and eight touchdowns in 2013, adding 845 kick return yards on the season. Beckham won a slew of awards his junior year, including the Paul Hornung Award, which is given to college football's most versatile athlete.

QUICK FACT

The 109-yard field goal return for a touchdown was a college football record that was tied a year later by Auburn's Chris Davis against Alabama in 2015.

Beckham finished his career at LSU with 4,118 all-purpose yards. That's good for fifth in school history. He also ranks ninth in school history in receptions (143) and seventh in receiving yards (2,340). But he did not return for his senior season, instead opting to enter the NFL Draft. The pros were calling.

CHAPTER TWO

The Rookie

Despite all his talent, Odell Beckham Jr. was not the first overall pick of the 2014 NFL Draft. That honor went to Jadeveon Clowney, a defensive end from the University of South Carolina who was taken by the Houston Texans. Beckham wasn't even the first wideout taken in the draft. That was Clemson wide receiver Sammy Watkins, who the Buffalo Bills traded up to take fourth overall. In fact, 11 teams passed on Beckham, who would go on to have one of the best rookie seasons for a receiver in NFL history.

But why? For some teams, the answer is simple: they weren't looking to draft a wideout that high. For others, especially teams who picked wide receivers that weren't Odell Beckham Jr., their picks would haunt their fans for years to come. The Cleveland Browns, for example, passed twice on taking Beckham. And wideouts like Watkins and Mike Evans (seventh overall, Tampa Bay) have not had nearly as successful careers as Beckham.

His size, for one, was an issue coming out of college. Beckham attended the NFL Scouting Combine and was tested for a variety of different attributes. He ran a 40-yard dash in 4.43 seconds. His draft profile

QUICK FACT

Jarvis Landry was taken with the second to last pick in the second round of the 2014 NFL Draft. He went 63rd overall to the Miami Dolphins.

Beckham poses with his mother at the 2014 NFL Draft.

Beckham was taken 14th overall by the New York Giants in the 2014 NFL Draft. He was not the first wideout picked, but once he took the field he proved to be one of the best receivers in the game.

projected him as a first or second round pick, but expectations were not particularly high for Beckham on the official scouting report.

Talented, competitive, productive, inconsistent college split end who projects as a flanker or slot receiver in the pros, where a creative offensive coordinator can take advantage of his run-after-catch skills. Could be a productive No. 3 option with added value as a kick returner.

Both Landry and Beckham entered the NFL Draft in the same year. Beckham was asked about what would happen if Landry were taken before him, though he didn't seem to mind.

"Jarvis is like a brother to me, so we just wish the best for each other," Beckham told reporters in 2014. "Honestly, whoever gets picked first you'll be sitting there clapping, and I just hope he does the best he can."

Beckham, though, was taken first. He was the 14th overall pick in the 2014 NFL Draft, chosen by the New York Giants. Despite his underwhelming draft combine profile, Beckham and the Giants were thrilled. He said it "couldn't have worked out any better" and called it a "perfect situation."

QUICK FACT

Odell Beckham Jr. actually wanted to challenge his mom to a race in the 40-yard dash after the NFL Scouting Combine! Today, she coaches track and field.

Delayed Start

Beckham's first days with the Giants were not easy. He hurt his hamstring and missed an extended period of time while recovering from the injury. It was a frustrating start for him and Giants head coach Tom Coughlin, who admitted that he was not happy with the receiver's health to start his pro career.

Beckham missed the first four games of his rookie season and still had one of the most productive rookie years in recent memory.

Beckham's injury lingered, and he missed the start of his rookie season and its first four games. He finally played in his first career NFL game on October 5, 2014, when the 2–2 Giants hosted the Atlanta Falcons. Beckham had four catches for 44 yards in his NFL debut. He also scored his first career NFL touchdown, a 15-yard pass from quarterback Eli Manning that helped the Giants win, 30–20.

Finally healthy, Beckham took off. Against the Indianapolis Colts, Beckham had 146 yards receiving and two touchdowns.

The Catch

In Week 12 of his rookie season, Odell Beckham Jr. made one of the greatest catches in NFL history. It happened on November 23, when the Giants hosted the Dallas Cowboys in a *Sunday Night Football* game. On the first play of the second quarter with the Giants leading 7–3, Giants quarterback Eli Manning rolled out and threw a long pass down the right sideline to the end zone. Beckham leaped up at the goal line, extended his right hand high over his back, and somehow snagged the pass.

There was actually a penalty called on the play, as Cowboys cornerback Brandon Carr interfered with Beckham. But Beckham caught it anyway, getting both feet and even a hand down in bounds while holding onto the ball with his other hand for the touchdown.

"How in the world?" NBC announcer Bob Costas asked. "I mean, he is ... insane. How do you make that catch?"

QUICK-FACT

Beckham and New York Giants quarterback Eli Manning went to the same high school. Manning had actually thrown to Beckham once when he visited the school while the wideout was on the football team!

"The Catch" on November 23, 2014, made Beckham a household name. With that attention, however, came some challenges.

His fellow sportscaster, Cris Collinsworth, gushed about the catch as well. "That might be the greatest catch I've ever seen," the former wideout said.

Others on the field agreed with those in the broadcast booth. "I have played this game for 10 years," Giants safety Antrel Rolle said after the game, "and that was the greatest catch I've seen."

Afterward, Beckham tried to downplay the significance of the catch. "I hope it is not the greatest catch," Beckham told the Associated Press, "because with time I hope I can make more."

Many people, including basketball superstar LeBron James, did rave about Beckham's catch. "Man I just witnessed the greatest catch ever possibly," James said on Twitter. "WOW!!!!"

The catch was so famous that the Pro Football Hall of Fame put the jersey Beckham wore in the game on display later in 2014.

Honor Roll

"The Catch," as it became known, was the highlight of what was a remarkable rookie season for Beckham. He led the league with 108.8

Beckham won the Associated Press's award for Offensive Rookie of the Year in 2014.

receiving yards per game. Beckham finished with 91 catches for 1,305 yards receiving and had 12 touchdowns. He won the Pro Football Writers Association and Associated Press Offensive Rookie of the Year awards. Beckham was also elected to play in the Pro Bowl as a rookie.

But after the season Beckham admitted that, as good a year as he had, he had a "long process" to recover from his hamstring injury after the season and get fully healthy.

"I was never fully healthy," Beckham told ESPN in January 2015. "I was just trying to manage it and maintain it … It's still not right. [I'm] still working on it."

In other words, the best for Beckham was yet to come. If he could stay on the field.

CHAPTER THREE

Growing Pains

Expectations were high for Odell Beckham Jr.'s second season with the New York Giants. The wideout had set the NFL record for the best first 12 games in a receiver's pro career. Beckham was unsatisfied, and rightfully so. He battled injuries and the Giants didn't make the playoffs, but there was plenty of reason to be optimistic.

"I felt the year went well," Beckham told ESPN that offseason. "There's still so much I can look back on and say, I wish I had done that or I wish I had done this. But it was great to get in and to be able to learn and experience things and just get a year of experience under my belt."

His sophomore effort with the Giants did not come without controversy, though. Beckham was outstanding, putting up more huge receiving numbers for the team. On the season, Beckham had 96 catches for 1,450 receiving yards, good for fifth in the league. He also had 13 touchdowns, including a season-long 87-yard score against the New England Patriots on November 15, 2015.

QUICK FACT

In 2015, New Orleans Saints quarterback Drew Brees helped Beckham set a world record for the most one-handed catches in a minute. Beckham caught 33 balls, but the record has since been broken.

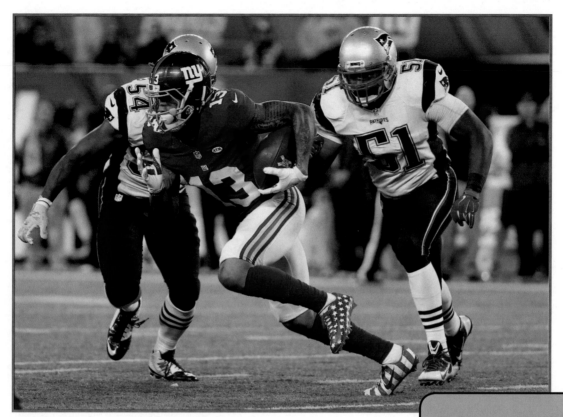

Losing His Cool

Beckham's sophomore season in the NFL brought more records, but it also brought on-field controversy.

But the most notable event in his 2015 season came against the Carolina Panthers in Week 15. Beckham had just six catches for 76 yards in the game on December 20, all in the second half. He dropped two passes in the first half and was defended by cornerback Josh Norman, a standout defender for the Panthers. A frustrated Beckham became increasingly violent in his battles with Norman as the game went on, and officials began to take notice.

In the third quarter, Beckham made a catch and was tackled by Norman. He swatted at Norman after the play and was given a personal foul penalty. Minutes later, on a Shane Vereen run, Beckham launched himself at Norman as he tried to tackle the Giants running

Beckham has let his anger get the best of him on the field, which has drawn a lot of attention over the years.

back. Beckham got another penalty, one of four he received on the day.

The Panthers took a 35–7 lead in the game, but the Giants stormed back. Some were surprised that Beckham was not kicked out of the game. He was called "out of control" by Fox broadcaster Joe Buck. But Beckham was allowed to keep playing. In fact, he later caught a game-tying touchdown in the fourth quarter. The Panthers, though, did pull out the win.

Beckham was suspended one game for the incident, and he missed the Giants' Week 16 game against the Minnesota Vikings. It was the second time that season that Beckham was punished for actions he took during a game. In Week 4, Beckham was fined $9,000 after players on the Buffalo Bills alleged that he threw punches multiple times during the game.

Beckham appealed the suspension but lost, later posting an apology on Twitter and through a team statement: "A lot of kids look up to me as a role model. That is a responsibility I accept and take seriously. Many of the parents of those kids have

Beckham (*center*) helps at the tryouts for the Triple Shot Challenge: Kids' Choice Sports $50,000 Perfect Pass Challenge in 2016. Beckham said he knows how important it is to be a role model for young people, and he has tried to improve his behavior on the field.

asked since Sunday what they should say to their children about my conduct. I don't have the perfect answer, but … when you act like that, there are consequences. And I hope to be an example of somebody who did something wrong and learned from it."

The Giants would finish a disappointing 6–10, and Coughlin would leave the team after the season.

New Year, More Trouble

Beckham returned with the Giants in 2016 under new head coach Ben McAdoo. But his battles with Norman were still discussed heading into the

Washington Redskins cornerback Josh Norman breaks up a pass to Beckham in September 2016. Beckham's public battles with Norman have taken place on and off the field.

new season. In the offseason, Norman signed with Washington, which meant the two would square off against each other twice a year.

Norman claimed he picked the Washington Redskins because they are "a team on the rise." But he and Beckham later sparred on Twitter, and Norman even wrote about the incident in his own *Players' Tribune* story. Beckham addressed it in a *GQ* cover story that summer, saying he was "sure" Norman signed with Washington to play Beckham more often.

"If I wasn't playing him twice a year, maybe people wouldn't bring it up as much," Beckham told the magazine. "But now it'll be a lot more media attention for him, attention that I don't really look for, attention that I don't need. The reason that he's become so relevant is because of me."

He did call the fight against Norman "the one blemish" on his career, and he seemed eager to challenge him on the field.

The 2016 season was a big improvement for the Giants as a team. They went 11–5 and made the playoffs for the first time in Beckham's career. He was also criticized for taking out his frustrations on a kicking net on the sideline in a Week 3 matchup against Josh Norman and Washington. Despite that, Beckham finished with 101 receptions on the season and 1,367 yards with 10 receiving touchdowns on the year.

The Giants' season ended in Green Bay on Wild Card weekend, with the Packers winning 38–13 over New York. The team, especially Beckham, got criticized by fans and the New York media after photos emerged of Giants wideouts spending time in Florida on an off day between the last game of the regular season and the playoff matchup against the Packers.

Beckham also reportedly punched a wall at Lambeau Field in frustration after the loss

QUICK FACT

Beckham wears number 13 on his Giants jersey. Other Giants players who have worn that number previously are punter Dave Jennings, quarterbacks Jared Lorenzen, Danny Kanell, and Kurt Warner, and wideout Ramses Barden.

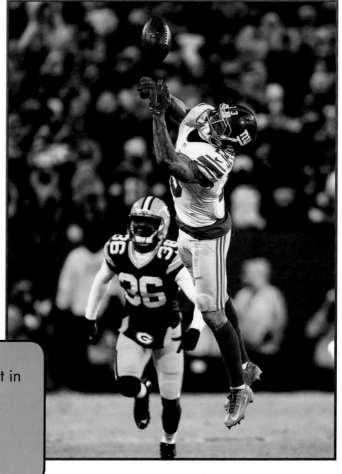

Beckham and the Giants fell short in a 2016 NFC Wild Card Game against the Green Bay Packers, which led to more drama for the wide receiver and his team.

to the Packers. He commented about both after the game, saying he regrets the attention the trip to Florida caused for his team.

"All the extra attention and distraction it caused our team and our organization, I don't think any of us wanted that and that's where the regrets may lie," Beckham told ESPN.

In just three seasons, Beckham had set 13 Giants franchise records and 20 individual NFL records, including the fastest ever to attain 3,500 yards receiving. But success in the postseason had been tough to find, and many wondered if he was too immature to become a leader.

Soccer, Fashion, and Beyond

Beckham loves other sports beyond football and is actually a huge soccer fan. His idol growing up was English soccer player David Beckham. Though he was no relation to Beckham, the wideout said he used to joke that he was family and said he was "like a little kid" when he finally got to meet him.

David Beckham (*center*) of the LA Galaxy plays in a soccer match against Real Madrid in 2012. Odell Beckham Jr. said his sports idol is the now-retired soccer star.

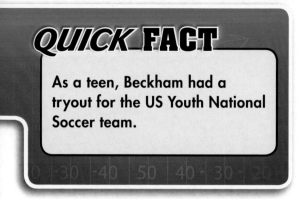

"I got to meet one of my childhood idols since I could ever remember, and a guy who I watched probably since I was four or five years old," Beckham said in 2015. "It was a pretty surreal moment for me, meeting a guy who I've clowned about being a relative of all this time."

Odell Beckham Jr. said the soccer star gave him some good advice, too. "He just told me, 'You have to keep the legacy going,'" Beckham Jr. said. "He told me he was watching me throughout the season, catching bits and pieces of it in London or L.A., wherever he's at. But he's been keeping up with me and watching me, and just to keep up the family name."

Beckham is a big soccer fan in general, and he lists David Alaba as his favorite player. Alaba, an Austrian who plays for German club Bayern Munich, considers Odell Beckham Jr. his friend, and the two often hang out when they are not playing for their clubs.

Fashion Forward

One of Odell Beckham's defining characteristics off the field is his sense of style. In 2016, Beckham designed his own fashion line, which went on sale at the department store Bloomingdales. He calls himself a fashion icon, and *Sports Illustrated* gave him its "swag award" when it named its best dressed athletes in 2017.

Even his hairstyle has become popular thanks to his outstanding play on the field. In fact, his famous catch from his rookie season helped make the look—close-shaved head on the sides and longer dyed blonde hair on top—a popular look with younger football fans.

"It's always flattering when people, especially kids, want to copy your style," Beckham said in 2015, according to *Sports Illustrated*. "For me, I just like the look."

Beckham has been placed on *Sports Illustrated*'s best dressed athletes list. Beckham has even started designing his own clothes.

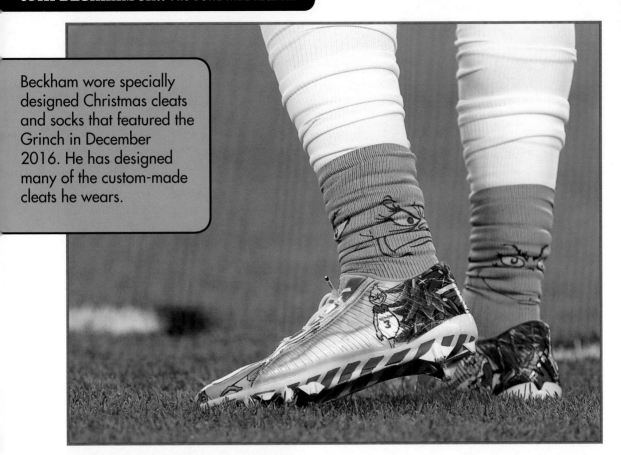

Beckham wore specially designed Christmas cleats and socks that featured the Grinch in December 2016. He has designed many of the custom-made cleats he wears.

QUICK FACT

Beckham calls himself a "sneakerhead," or someone who loves sneakers and collects them.

Beyond fashion, Beckham spends a lot of time working with the Make-A-Wish Foundation to help children. His cleats—which he usually designs—are often auctioned off for charity and to benefit causes he feels close to.

The Bright Future?

The 2017 season was supposed to be a chance for Beckham to settle in with a Giants team attempting to shake off a bad postseason performance. His fifth-year option was picked up by the Giants, meaning he would stay with the club until at least 2019. But it was also a difficult

Beckham returns a punt for a touchdown against the Detroit Lions on December 18, 2016. However, the play was called back on a holding penalty. The Giants struggled in the 2016–17 season.

one for Beckham and the league as a whole. Beckham injured his left ankle during preseason against the Cleveland Browns. The injury made him a surprise scratch for the team's season-opener against the Cowboys.

Beckham returned in Week 2 against the Detroit Lions, but the team struggled and lost again. In Week 3, Beckham scored two touchdowns but drew ire for a touchdown celebration in which he got down on all fours and mimicked a dog relieving himself. Beckham was fined for the incident and Giants ownership was reportedly upset with the celebration.

Once again, fans and people in the media called for Beckham to mature and move past controversy in his life. It's a cry that's followed him throughout his NFL career thus far and one that will only die down if he ceases such behavior in the future.

Beckham is a player who has played through some gruesome injuries and played outstanding football despite the pain. The next week, he dislocated his finger on a pass from Eli Manning. He left the game, then returned to the lineup after the finger was popped back into place.

Beckham posted a photo on social media of the exact moment the pass dislocated his finger, a striking example of the kind of sacrifices NFL players make to play through pain.

"I give this game everything I got," Beckham wrote in 2017. "Ain't no way around it."

Injuries struck Beckham again in Week 5, this time ending his 2017 season. After a 48-yard touchdown and 97 yards in the game, Beckham fractured his left ankle during the Giants' 27–22 loss to the Los Angeles Chargers. He was carted off the field and appeared to be crying. Beckham later had surgery on the ankle and was placed on injured reserve.

It was the most disappointing season yet for Beckham, who played in only four games and had 25 catches for 302 yards and three touchdowns. But

Beckham played through multiple injuries in 2017 until a broken leg during the October 8, 2017, game against the Los Angeles Chargers ended his season.

as he reaffirmed in his Instagram post days before his season-ending injury, Beckham has proven he does work hard and is dedicated to football. He's able to catch footballs one-handed because he's constantly working on it in practice. It's not just sticky gloves or luck that make him as good as he is: it's something he's worked at all his life.

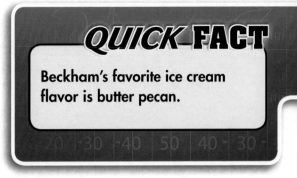

QUICK FACT

Beckham's favorite ice cream flavor is butter pecan.

His father feels that his son will grow as his career continues. "I asked Odell what his goals were in terms of football and his response was 'legendary,'" Beckham Sr. explained. "Legendary extends beyond football. I'm glad he understands that his influence reaches off the field and he has an opportunity most people do not get."

That hope is shared by many Giants fans and others in the league that want to see Beckham continue the incredible start he's had to his career. But being a great NFL player is more than just the numbers that make up one's statistics. If Beckham is to continue growing as a superstar in the NFL, the hope is that he grows in other areas as well.

TIMELINE

1992: Odell Beckham Jr. is born on November 5, in Baton Rouge, Louisiana.

2011: On January 8, Beckham commits to playing football for Louisiana State University. On September 3, he plays his first game as a freshman for the Tigers.

2013: On September 7, Beckham scores on a 109-yard missed field goal return for a touchdown against the University of Alabama at Birmingham.

2014: On May 8, Beckham is taken 14th overall in the NFL Draft by the New York Giants. On May 19, Beckham signs a contract with the Giants. On October 5, he plays in his first game with the Giants. On November 23, Beckham makes "The Catch" on *Sunday Night Football* against the Dallas Cowboys. On December 8, Beckham's jersey from "The Catch" is put on display at the Pro Football Hall of Fame.

2015: On January 7, Beckham is named to his first Pro Bowl. On January 30, he sets a new world record with 33 one-handed catches in a minute. In May, Beckham is named EA Sports *Madden NFL 16* cover athlete. On December 20, Beckham fights with Josh Norman in a Week 15 game against the Panthers, and on the following day, he is suspended for one game.

2016: Beckham announces his own fashion line at Bloomingdales department store.

2017: On January 8, the New York Giants lose Beckham's first playoff game to the Green Bay Packers. On April 24, the Giants pick up Beckham's fifth-year option. In July, Beckham is named to *Sports Illustrated*'s best dressed athlete list and wins the "swag award." On September 10, he misses the first game of the 2017 season with an ankle injury. On September 17, Beckham is flagged for a touchdown celebration and draws ire from the New York Giants' management. On October 8, Beckham fractures his left ankle in a game against the Los Angeles Chargers and has surgery on the following day.

Tom Brady (1977–) is one of the greatest quarterbacks in NFL history. He's the only player to win five Super Bowls with the same team. A four-time Super Bowl MVP, he owns many different passing records and is a 12-time Pro Bowl selection.

DeMarcus Ware (1982–) is a Super Bowl champion, and he played outside linebacker and defensive end for the Dallas Cowboys from 2005–13 and Denver Broncos from 2014–16. A nine-time Pro Bowler, he was named to the NFL 2000s All-Decade Team, and the governor of Alabama made April 19, 2016, "DeMarcus Ware Day."

Aaron Rodgers (1983–) is one of the most accurate passers in NFL history. Rodgers led the Green Bay Packers to a Super Bowl victory in 2011 and was named Super Bowl MVP. He has been named league MVP twice and is a six-time Pro Bowl selection.

Antonio Brown (1988–) is one of the most prolific wideouts in the game today. Brown, who plays with the Pittsburgh Steelers, has made the Pro Bowl five times and has been First Team All-Pro three times in his career. He led the league in receptions in 2014 and 2015 and led the league in receiving yards in 2014 with 1,698 yards.

Russell Wilson (1988–) is a quarterback with the Seattle Seahawks, who led his team to the divisional round of the 2012 playoffs and was named Rookie of the Year. He also tied a record for most passing touchdowns by a rookie quarterback. Wilson led the Seahawks to their first Super Bowl title in 2014. A Pro Bowler, Wilson was the first quarterback in NFL history to throw three or more passing touchdowns and no interceptions in five consecutive games and has one of the highest completion percentages in league history.

Julio Jones (1989–) is an explosive wideout with the Atlanta Falcons. Jones had a dominant collegiate career at Alabama before reaching the NFL. Jones is a four-time Pro Bowl selection and two-time All-Pro. In 2016, Jones led the Falcons to a Super Bowl and had 300 receiving yards in a single game.

Cam Newton (1989–) is one of the most dynamic and toughest quarterbacks in the game. Newton is a Heisman Trophy winner, and the Carolina Panthers selected him with the first overall pick in the 2011 NFL Draft. He led the Panthers to the Super Bowl in 2016. Newton was named league MVP in 2015 and holds the NFL record for the most rushing touchdowns by a quarterback in a single season.

Rob Gronkowski (1989–) is a two-time Super Bowl champion, a four-time Pro Bowler, and one of the most dangerous tight ends in NFL history. He has been playing tight end for the New England Patriots since being drafted in 2010. His size and strength at the position has revolutionized the way modern offenses play football.

GLOSSARY

all-purpose yards The total amount of yards a player has gained through receiving, rushing, or returning punts and kickoffs in football.

dislocate To move a bone out of its normal location or position in a joint.

downplay To make something seem smaller or less important.

fifth-year option Part of an NFL rookie contract that allows a team to keep the player for a fifth season.

fracture To cause a crack or break in something hard, such as a bone.

franchise A team that is a member of a professional sports league.

gruesome Causing horror or disgust.

inconsistent Not always acting or behaving in the same way.

injured reserve A designation for a player who is injured and cannot play for a professional team.

ire Intense anger.

NFL Draft An annual event in which NFL teams select college football players to play for them.

NFL Scouting Combine A weeklong event where college football players show their mental and physical skills to NFL teams who may be looking to draft them.

Pro Bowl The NFL's version of an all-star game in which the players are voted on by coaches, fans, and their peers.

showcase To show off in a very attractive or favorable way.

slot receiver A player split out wide on the football field between the quarterback and the wideout furthest to the sideline; often the third-best receiver on the team.

Super Bowl The annual championship game in the NFL between the top teams from the American Football Conference and the National Football Conference.

underwhelming Failing to be impressive.

versatile Able to be used in many different ways.

wideout An offensive football player who may catch a forward pass; also known as a receiver or wide receiver.

Books

Blumberg, Saulie. *New York Giants*. Minneapolis, MN: SportsZone, 2017.

Bowker, Paul. *Odell Beckham Jr.* Minneapolis, MN: SportsZone, 2018.

Burgess, Zack. *Meet the New York Giants*. Chicago, IL: Norwood House Press, 2017.

Fishman, Jon M. *Odell Beckham Jr.* Minneapolis, MN: Lerner Publications, 2017.

Gigliotti, Jim. *The Pro Football Draft*. Broomall, PA: Mason Crest, 2017.

Gitlin, Marty. *Odell Beckham Jr.: Football Star*. Lake Elmo, MN: Focus Readers, 2017.

Gray, Aaron Jonathan. *Football Record Breakers*. Minneapolis, MN: SportsZone, 2016.

Karras, Steven M. *New York Giants*. New York, NY: AV2, 2018.

Kelley, K. C. *Football Superstars 2017*. Santa Barbara, CA: Beach Ball Books, 2017.

Lyon, Drew. *A Superfan's Guide to Pro Football Teams*. North Mankato, MN: Capstone Press, 2018.

Mack, Larry. *The New York Giants Story*. Minneapolis, MN: Bellwether Media, 2017.

Nagelhout, Ryan. *20 Fun Facts About Football*. New York, NY: Gareth Stevens Publishing, 2016.

Scheff, Matt. *Superstars of the New York Giants*. Mankato, MN: Amicus High Interest, 2014.

Websites

ESPN
http://www.espn.com/nfl/player/_/id/16733/odell-beckham-jr

National Football League
http://www.nfl.com/player/odellbeckham/2543496/profile

New York Giants
http://www.giants.com/team/roster/Odell-Beckham%20Jr/
    e6fdc468-f493-4b1c-b597-705977b6f195
Facebook: @odell.beckham; Instagram: @obj; Twitter: @OBJ_3

INDEX

Manning, Eli, 20, 21, 38
McAdoo, Ben, 29
Mettenberger, Zach, 13, 14
Miami Dolphins, 16
Minnesota Vikings, 27

N

New England Patriots, 24
New Orleans, 9
New Orleans Saints, 24
New York Giants, 4, 6, 19, 20, 24, 25,
    27, 29, 31, 32, 36, 37, 38, 39
NFL Draft, 15, 16, 19
NFL Scouting Combine, 19
Norman, Josh, 25, 29–30, 31
North Texas, 11

O

O'Neal, Shaquille, 9
Oregon Ducks, 11

P

Paul Hornung Award, 15
Pro Football Hall of Fame, 22
Pro Football Writers Association Offensive
    Rookie of the Year, 23

S

Seattle Seahawks, 6
Sherman, Richard, 6
Sunday Night Football, 4, 20

T

Tampa Bay, 16
touchdown celebrations, 4, 37
Towson University, 11
track, 7, 9

U

University of Alabama Birmingham, 14
University of South Carolina, 16
US Army All-American Bowl, 9

V

Vereen, Shane, 25
Von Norman, Heather (mother), 7, 9, 19

W

Washington Redskins, 30, 31
Watkins, Sammy, 16
West Virginia, 11
Wild Card weekend, 31